John Fulton

The Dual Revolutions

Anti-slavery and pro-slavery

John Fulton

The Dual Revolutions
Anti-slavery and pro-slavery

ISBN/EAN: 9783337235666

Printed in Europe, USA, Canada, Australia, Japan

Cover: Foto ©ninafisch / pixelio.de

More available books at **www.hansebooks.com**

THE DUAL REVOLUTIONS.

ANTI-SLAVERY

AND

PRO-SLAVERY.

BY S. M. JOHNSON.

BALTIMORE:
PRINTED BY W. M. INNES,
ADAMS EXPRESS BUILDING.

1863.

THE DUAL REVOLUTIONS.

He who shall succeed in writing a perfect history of
American Abolitionism, including its last great triumph,
under Mr. Lincoln's new government—he, who shall succeed in a perfect analysis of the measures and teachings of
that pestilent brood of fanatics and madmen, and shall
trace out and record their efforts to overthrow the government of the Union, will merit the applause of his country,
and the approbation of posterity. It is not the purpose of
these few pages to accomplish this formidable work. They
are designed only as a sort of reconnoissance—a prelimi-
nary survey of the ground—and perhaps, to remove some
of the obstructions which impede the progress of historical
and critical investigation. It is an ungrateful task; because it involves the exposure of measures and combinations, not only discreditable to the immediate parties
thereto, but to the whole American people, who, at least,
have been silent witnesses of their progress. The seat of
these infamous combinations is in New England. It is
New England that has sent down that horde of Appenine
wolves, which have torn the Union to atoms, and are now
feeding on its vitals. That the great public is blameless,
cannot be maintained. That they are, to a certain extent,
responsible for the evils which now afflict the nation, no
rational mind will deny. Their crime is that of submission, rather than of aggression;—that of being deceived
and misled, rather than of willful heresy to the Union, and
dishonest refusal to fulfill its obligations.

We have caused the rebellion. 1. By subverting the
government. 2. By our overbearing, insolent and tyran-
nizing tendencies.

A great people we are; it required a great people to do
what we have done, to sacrifice what we have sacrificed, in
blood and money. Our merits are great, and our errors
and crimes are great. I never thought our people as perfect as they thought themselves. We had an admirable
system of labor and laws. Under these, capital was widely
distributed, energy concentrated, and the interests of the
great body of the people promoted. This distribution of
wealth energized the nation and made it capable of greater
acts and greater sacrifices, than any other. It did not so

much enlighten and elevate the mind, as strengthen the
body. It enabled us to provide wonderful means; because,
in respect to the production of means, no other nation ever
employed a tithe of the intelligence, which has been employed in such production, in the States of the North. The
truth is, the minds of our people have all been used *to make
money.* The transitions from poverty to competence, and
back again, are as sudden and as rapid as the shifting
scenes of the stage. We have given little time and reflection to politics, as a principle, and much to politics as
a trade. The amenities of social and political life have
not only been neglected, but treated as weaknesses to be
avoided or condemned. The character of the government
is less understood now than it was fifty years ago. This
decline in political knowledge has opened the way for the
introduction into it of every conceivable heresy. When
the present struggle commenced, it found us not only pro-
foundly ignorant of the system we felt called upon to save,
but of quite all the rules and principles of civilized warfare.
We regarded the first signal of disturbance as an edict of
excommunication of *all* the slave States, treated the people
thereof as outlaws, and sought, with a sort of fiendish
relish for blood, to exterminate them.

Nine millions of Southerners suddenly found themselves,
not only disfranchised, but hunted with all the hounds of
war *for extermination!* That was disunion. That was the
seal of the covenant of dissolution. That was the proof
which we offered up to all the world, that, however
rich we might be in resources—in schools and colleges—
we were sadly poor in civilization, policy, humanity and
good practical sense. We wanted to fight, in order that
we might exterminate the rebels. We would not have an
accommodation of differences; because we were strong
enough to put them down, and we wanted the satisfaction
of doing it with a sort of ante-christian vengeance! It was
in fact the right arm of the North—so we thought—which
constituted the government of the Union. It was very
insolence, in anybody, to question the power of that arm.
It could hardly endure the existence of the States. There
was rivalry in the States. We could not brook the thought
that there should be any other governing power on this
continent, than the Union. The South dared to think
differently; and she must be punished. We raised
armies—great armies—to put the South down—literally
to put the South down! The North was all loyal—the
South was all disloyal, and they were disloyal to the best
government, and the best public opinion, in the world—
the immaculate judgment and public opinion, of the North!
As the North was great and good, so the South was evil-

minded, contentious, wicked—outlaws. They had offended, even in contending for their rights; for the North was better than the Union—better than the Constitution. They were rich, powerful and almost omnipotent. They were humane, philanthropic and religious. They recognized, to be sure, the forms of the Federal Constitution ; but they had advanced a few steps above all human contrivances of the kind, where they discerned a higher and a better law. This law, it was their duty to enforce, just as it is the duty of the Christian missionary, to enlighten the heathen and convert the infidel. The South was the great Heathen in the sight of the Northern mind. She must be converted—she must have the atonement of blood—the reconciliation of slaughter. We must inflict heavy wounds upon all her people, and then set our surgeons at work to bandage them up. At least it would advance the science of surgical anatomy! Felons are given up to the dissectors. The South were all felons. They had rebelled against the North. They ventured even to think their morality was as good as the North. They dared to question the philanthropy of the abolitionist, and to suggest that the field of genuine benevolence amongst the poor of the free States was broad enough, and inviting enough, to occupy all their men and means. That was a great offence. Resistance was nothing but impudence and insolence. There was no actual criminality in rebellion, because the power to crush it was complete. The crime consisted in holding slaves. That was the *corpus delicti*. We punish the criminal for what he does, not for what he said, when arrested, or even for his actions under arrest. The offence consisted, in fact, in violating our higher law, which prohibits slavery. It was aggravated by assumptions of equality with us, in morals, in religion, and even politics. Before our new dispensation, the South was our equal; when we passed under the full blaze of its enlightening power, they became our wards. We had believed, with them, in the efficacy of constitutions of government—in the equality of all the States, as members of the Union—in the sovereign right of each State to regulate its own internal polity, in its own way. That was under the old covenant—when we were all heathens together. Light broke in upon us, but not upon the South. That was what divided us. It sent us ahead and them backwards.

These observations are put forth with a view of defining the position of the parties; as one would present the law that has been violated before demanding the conviction of the culprit. The people constitute the tribunal before whom the law and the facts should be fairly stated. It is as much the interest of good men to protect the innocent as to punish the guilty. The country accuses Mr. Lincoln's government of high crimes. If the people of the North have blundered and sinned, that is no reason why Mr. Lincoln and Mr. Seward should do the same. They were elected to office in the conviction that they were statesmen. To be less than statesmen, was to assure the failure of the administration to do its duty ; and this, in such times, is a crime. Mistakes are crimes. To do too little is a crime. To do too much is a crime.

The administration commenced their work by over-estimating the power of the North, and under-estimating that of the South. They imbibed the popular notion that numbers are everything—that numbers have more strength, more money, more material, more mind than what Mr. Lincoln would call lesser numbers; and that numbers, including material, are ubiquitous. This was not the only blunder; they regarded numbers as the government. The Constitution they proposed to protect and defend, was the popular Hue and Cry. They knew no other law. They imagined, that obeying the impulse of the nation, they were safe. That impulse they did obey; and there their obedience ceased : in all else, they set up for themselves. The house was in disorder, and they could run riot in theft, plunder and murder. Anarchy does not call people to account, it does not punish crime ; it makes it.

The fruits of this species of political ethics are the same in all climates, in all places and amongst every people. They are sweet to the first taste, but grow bitter, repulsive and intolerable to the second. The power that oppresses is imposing and even agreeable to all save its victims. One by one these are numbered till the majority have suffered. Then the fruit becomes bitter—insufferably bitter. The people denounce what they a few months before applauded to the echo. To be practical as well as speculative, Mr. Lincoln's government, a year ago, though the worst in the world, was the most popular. More was done for it, less was required of it : more was said in its praise, less was done to deserve it, than any other government. Everything was wrong ; it was wrong in its spirit—wrong in its principles, wrong in its policy, wrong in its acts—it was wrong in everything. It was right in nothing, save that it did unquestionably represent the impulse of the people of the North. We elected Mr. Lincoln to be President of the United States—to be the head of a government of laws—of a perfectly organized system ; he became the President of an ill-omened, ranting impulse. We thought he had a sober-minded, clear-headed constituency : whether he had or not, those were the qualities we expected him to exhibit. The people did not swear, like Mr. Lincoln, to " protect and defend " the Constitution. They entrusted everything to him. They made the laws that they might be shielded against the evils of their own passions and impulses. They preferred a government to a mob. They made Mr. Lincoln President of their government; and he became the presiding genius of their mob. He heard only the Hue and Cry; and this gave him a mortal hatred to the judiciary. The judiciary is the antipode of the mob. It is the medicine administered to the sick body politic. It is offensive to the people only when they turn back to destroy themselves. Mr. Lincoln became the leader of a grand *emeute* where the people turned back upon themselves. His logic led him to say: " It is better to build a new house than repair the old one." The improvidence of passion is proverbial. Seeing it required but a moment to destroy, he imagined a moment would be enough to rebuild. He tore down the old house of our fathers, and left us shelterless— such of us as his evil mind did not put into the out-houses —the forts and prisons—of the old constitutional castle.

That we had serious difficulties to contend with, when Mr. Lincoln came into office, all admit. They required a steady hand, and an honest heart, to keep them under the control of peaceful remedies. They had been of slow, but malicious, origin and growth. They embraced a radical, but purely artificial, antagonism, between the great North and the great South. It is a singular feature in the intercourse of men that, while the union of Northern and Southern labor has produced the highest conditions of prosperity and happiness, it has ever been the source of individual differences, contentions and strife. All wealth is the net product of labor. In tropical regions, where the soil is fruitful and products command ready markets at high rates, the profits of labor are vastly greater than in more northern latitudes. This difference is principally due to two causes: 1. The expenses of labor in the warm climates are much less than in the cold. 2. The peculiar products of the former command more universal markets than the latter. The great consuming populations of the earth inhabit the colder regions, where, in order to meet the rigors of climate, more is required to sustain animal existence. Hence it is that in estimating the grand productions of a people, the question of climate is considered, for animals, throughout their entire range, are consumers. The census presents the total production of hay and its value, and it is found, perhaps, to equal that of cotton and its value. The former is an article of animal consumption. It is raised for the very purpose of sustaining the animal economy, indirectly for the benefit of man; while cotton is an article adapted to the direct use of man. So of sugar; so of rice; so of

coffee ; so of tobacco ; and so of quite all the products of
the tropical regions. These interesting facts prove most con-
clusively that there is no real antagonism between the North
and the South. What, then, is the ground of difference?
It is a question of temperament, and, consequently, of
intellect and morals. The North are more phlegmatic.
They are a cold, calculating, industrious, frugal race. Their
industry, economy and frugality have made them rich ; for
they have wonderful enterprise, and have laid all the world
under contribution to their enterprise. They have, for
more than a century past, been the machinists, the manufacturers, the factors, the capitalists, the school teachers,
the inventors, the engineers, and, to a great extent, the
lawyers, doctors and mechanics of the South. The profits
accruing to the North through these sources are beyond cal-
culation. Profits are in the foreground of every picture of
Northern enterprise. That is the principle, the policy and
the law of Northern society. Nor is it to be deprecated
when kept within the bounds of reason. It is only the insolence of wealth and the trickery of enterprise that we
would condemn. If the North have an excess of the coun-
terfeit, the South are sadly deficient in the genuine. There
is no antagonism between the honest labor of the two regions
—none between the honest minds of the two regions. It
is the corrupt, the ambitious, the sinister, the fraudulent,
the self-opiniated and Fanatical men of the two sections, between whom there is a gulf of separation. These latter
parties have got the control ; and, getting it, they of the
North pointed with insolent manner to their majorities,
their power, their numbers and their money ! These were
the weapons to adjust questions of difference ; for differences, with low minds, beget thoughts of dominion. Numbers and muscle were, in the view of Mr. Lincoln's government, the proper instruments to be wielded : the
North was stronger than the South ! The question
was no longer whether the Union should be maintained ; it
was, whether numbers and money, should have dominion
over Mr. Lincoln's lesser numbers and money. The sober
minds of the nation wanted the old government in all its
integrity. They wanted it for what it had done and for
what they knew it could do. They wanted it for its memories and its benefits. They knew that justice alone could
restore it—stern political justice. There was no justice
outside of the compact that formed the Union. Our real
differences were all political—we were rent asunder by
opinions. It was opinions that divided us—opinions that
violated the Constitution. The North condemned slavery.
That was the right of the North. It was the opinion of the
North. The only question was how that opinion should

be exercised and where. It assumed the most offensive and aggressive form—it assailed the compact of Union. It abrogated its covenants. It denounced its morality. It raised up against it a higher law—a law that absolved the people from allegiance to their own Constitution. It interposed the power of Sovereign States to obstruct the enforcement of the constitutional rights of the citizens of other sovereign States. It created and legalized secession by denying the sovereignty of the Union over the interests delegated to the United States.

It was anti-slavery Opinion that did all this. It inaugurated revolution—and it was organic, radical, and successful revolution. It was successful; because, in its very nature, it destroyed the integrity of the government; and this was done by the States which created it. A lesser infraction could not have touched the integrity of the system—a lesser infraction could not have violated the letter of the compact. It required the parties to the government—the States—to impair the integrity of the Constitution. Impelled by anti-slavery Opinion, the States did violate the Constitution. They broke the law they had made, and had the power to amend or modify. The people of the North—the anti-slavery people of the North—the New England people of the North—violated, and did what they could to obliterate the spirit of the Union. They assumed to be better, to be wiser, more moral; more religious and humane, than the South. They were better, because they hated negro slavery; they were wiser, because they hated negro slavery; they were more moral and more religious for the same reason. No matter how good a people are, it is not well to boast of it; no matter how evil and deficient a people may be, it is not well to tell them of their faults and deficiencies. Where error exists the mind must be enlightened without offending the pride—without wounding the sensibilities. If the South were in error, it was bad policy and bad morals to correct them, by violating a compact we had entered into with them. Bad faith is a poor remedy, at best, for moral evils. There was no others complained of by the North. The Constitution recognized slavery; that was the evil. The North recognized slavery by being parties to the Constitution. They agreed thereby to surrender fugitive slaves; they refused to fulfill this agreement, because slavery was wrong—a violation of their higher law. The South did not concur in the moral judgment of the North, and insisted upon the fulfillment of their constitutional obligations. The North was inexorable. They threw up barricades against the government—they piled up the rubbish of a quarter of a century of anti-slavery agitation. They denounced the Union, and they legislated against the Union. They made it penal to aid in the enforcement of a federal law, in opposition to their higher law—their Puritan anti-slavery opinion. They called *their* law, the law of liberty; and the law of the Union, the law of despotism. They preferred the mob to the latter—they raised up mobs to resist the execution of the latter. They assailed the government till its offices fell into their hands—till the government became anti-slavery—till their mob got control of it; then they came to its support. Before their advent, it was treason to maintain the Constitution; after their advent it was treason to oppose their administration. Their Opinion became the government—their mob became the government. The President came into office on this Opinion. He represented it. He organized armies to enforce it. He usurped powers to carry it into effect. This was his *coup d'etat.* This was the consummation of revolution. A new government was made by it—an anti-slavery government. They proscribed the Constitution that they might proscribe slavery. To put down slavery, it was necessary to put down the Constitution; because that great compact was made by independent States, and slavery was purely a State interest. There was no way to reach it without obliterating State lines, and abrogating State rights and institutions. The name and forms of the old system were retained. Names and forms are every thing with a mob. Popular passion and excitement do not respect principles and covenants; they violate them.

We thus have a view of Mr. Lincoln's statesmanship up to the present time. It has been eminently successful. It has accomplished more than he had a right to expect. Its management of the elements has been complete at every point. He has consummated a new government—a government of absolute powers. The question of its stability is another matter. It is based upon popular passions, cemented by bad faith, and enforced by the hand of power. It rests upon violated rights, is sustained by sacrificed estates, and can be maintained only by the force of arms. Resting upon no principle of American society; sanctioned by no recognized habit or thought; enforced by no authority which the sober second thought of this people has not condemned, I have no faith in its stability, and no doubt of its early and complete overthrow. Whatever may be said in behalf of the Old Union, and its adaptation to the ends of government, there can be no doubt of the indestructibility of the State systems. Thrown from their spheres by the violence of the political hurricane, when the storm shall subside, they will return to their orbits, under the great social and industrial laws, by which they have been governed for more than two centuries. The habits of this people, in this respect, are fixed beyond the power of revolution. They may, for a day, turn back upon themselves and destroy their own works; but the sober judgment of the nation will demand the restoration of the old system ; because there is not a vestige of American history, a thought, or a memory, which is not identified with it. There is not a monument, nor a name, in all past time, which does not plead for the rights and sanctify the deeds of the States. These recollections are interwoven into the very fabric of American society ; and Mr. Lincoln's new government has to contend against them all. They utter a silent, but eloquent protest, against the new order, at every turn of the eye and every reflection of the mind. He has the conscience of the nation against him. His path is strewn with wrecks of the past ; every one of which proclaims the violated rights of our countrymen. These sacrifices, it will be remembered, were made to give effect to anti-slavery Opinion. They are wonderful indeed. A peaceful and successful government ; a united, happy, and prosperous people ; a rich, enterprising, and great nation, offered up on the altar of a Utopian philanthropy ; a miserable scheme for elevating a race which has proven its utter incapacity to sustain the responsibilities, and reap the benefits, of civilized life.

But the end is not yet. The wheel revolves on its axis. Mr. Lincoln and his Puritan cohorts were uppermost a few months ago. They are now descending. They have been successful, wonderfully successful. They have achieved a despotism without a dynasty. They have put in operation two revolutionary governments—that of the North and that of the South. The former, they created with their own hands. It is all their own ; the latter was created by the people of the South ; both are parts of the old wreck ; and measured by the standard of the Federal Constitution, both are illegitimate. That of the South, is sanctioned by the people it represents ; that of Mr. Lincoln, is sanctioned by the abolitionists. The former is an agency ; the latter is a usurpation. The one embodies the principles of popular government ; the other violates those principles. The one will live in its principles, though it should die in its forms ; the other will be hated and detested for its tyranny, though it should live in its forms.

But Mr. Lincoln's government has already failed. The popular Hue and Cry made it, the sober judgment of the nation has condemned it, and the popular Hue and Cry will destroy it. He repudiated the representative principle in its construction, but failed to inaugurate the dynastic principle which alone could perpetuate it. His genius was all adapted to pulling down the old system. He had no power to reconstruct a new one. A prodigal in the use of

power, he had no capacity to devise a scheme for its entail-
ment. He made a government for the North, which is
more detested and hated by the Northern people than that
of the South. He invaded the South with arms ; he invaded the North with a pensioned police, the miserable
dependants upon his power. He destroyed every safeguard
which had been provided for the protection of individuals.
He abrogated and annulled every institution erected by our
ancestors, between the Executive and the people. He
admitted the existence of such laws only as would strength-
en and enforce his authority. A venal Congress under
his absolute control, he did not wait even for the forms of
legislative sanction of his acts. Indecent haste to fortify
and consolidate his powers has marked every step of his
progress—every act of his government. Professing devotion to a system created for the protection of individuals
and property, he has swept away every guarantee of personal
rights, every pledge of personal security, and now exacts
from a subservient Congress an exculpatory law, relieving
him from the pains and penalties which our institutions
denounce against the violator of its laws. He thus inaugu-
rates the principle of Absolutism, by declaring that the
magistrate may violate, with impunity, the law he was
elected to enforce. He declares that the officer is not a
representative, but a dictator—that we are not citizens, but
subjects. He impeaches himself of high crimes committed
against the people, by meanly demanding exemption for
his illegal acts. A government so wanting in all the attributes of justice, fidelity and patriotism, could not command respect for its economical administration. In the
present case, whatever luxury has been able to effect in
wickedness, cruelty in punishment, pride in contumacy,
avarice in plunder, have been exhibited, at every point,
by Mr. Lincoln's government. Showing a want of fidelity
to his trusts, it is not wonderful that his example has been
followed by his dependants. Nor is the motive, in such
cases, to be separated from the act. He is a credulous and
weak man, who says Mr. Lincoln is honest in the pursuit
of an object, and dishonest in the use of means to attain it.
He who violates the law in one particular, ought not to be
entrusted with its execution in another. Honesty, in this
sense, degenerates into policy; and policy is dictated by dishonesty. This is the philosophy of despotism. When the
fountain is poisoned, it need not be counted that the stream
will be pure. Political infidelity, in the head of the State,
carries with it its corrupting power to all dependants.

Having thus stated the immediate process of our domestic
revolution, by reverting to the acts of the new government and the ends it has achieved, the picture must be en-

larged by adding a back ground, if for no other purpose
than to bring out the prominent figures into still more
positive relief. When the atmosphere becomes surcharged
with malignant vapors it invites and feeds the storm that
is to purify it. We have not suffered without cause. The
political hurricane that now propels its engines of destruction over our devoted country, is no freak or accident of
nature. We had violated the laws of justice, and are now
suffering the penalties imposed upon us. I have said that
our revolution was based on an opinion ; so it was. It
was anti-slavery Opinion, perfectly organized, and organized, too, in direct opposition to the government of the
Union. The result shows that it was stronger than the
Union. It elected Mr. Lincoln, in opposition to the Union—
in contempt of the Union. He was its candidate, and fail-
ing in faith to everything else, he has been, so far, the
President of this Opinion, and the enemy of the Union.
It is idle to contend for any other construction of the past.
Mr. Lincoln may profess friendship for the Union ; but
what say his acts ? Do they prove him to be sincere in
his attachment to that Constitution, which he violates at
every turn ? And what are the *tendencies* of these violations ? Do they not point, every one of them, as well by
their inherent character, as by the persons affected, to
Emancipation? Have we the old altars, the old ministers,
and the old ritual ? Do we believe in the efficacy of the
same principles? Is Mr. Lincoln, who tramples under
foot every maxim, usage, doctrine and covenant of the old
system, the President of the United States ? He has established a new standard of allegiance and imposed penalties
for its violation. Do these things bespeak his devotion to
the Constitution, and his determination to maintain it?
It is not his words, but his acts, that give us testimony.
Go to the public Forts erected to defend the people against
aggression from without ; let our imprisoned citizens tell
the story of their wrongs and oppressions. Ask for the
warrant under which they were incarcerated. Demand
the accusations against them. Publish the record. Read
from the Constitution, that "The right of the people to be
secure in their persons, houses, papers and effects, against
unreasonable searches and seizures shall not be violated,
and no warrant shall issue, but upon probable cause sup-
ported by oath or affirmation, and particularly describing
the place to be searched, and the *persons* or *things* to be
seized." That "no person shall be held to answer for a
capital or other infamous crime, unless on a presentment
or indictment of a Grand Jury, *except* in *cases* arising *in
the land or naval forces*, or *in the militia, when in actual
service in time of war or public danger*, *   *   * nor be

deprived of life, liberty or property *without* due process of
law"—and that "In all criminal prosecutions, the accused
shall enjoy the right to a speedy and public trial, by an
impartial jury of the State wherein the crime shall have
been committed, which district shall have been previously
ascertained by law, and to be informed of the nature and
cause of the accusation ; to be confronted with the witnesses against him ; to have compulsory process for ob-
taining witnesses in his favor, and to have the assistance
of counsel for his defense."

These covenants of the Constitution warrant the citizen
to arraign before the great tribunal of the nation, the vio-
lators of its laws. The culprits, though high in authority,
are amenable to this tribunal. They have perverted the
public trusts, committed to them, to ends of oppression and
wrong. They have exercised the powers, temporarily lodged
in their hands, for the purpose of preserving, protecting
and defending the institutions of the country, to destroy
those institutions, and deprive the people of life, liberty and
property, without cause, and without warrant or process of
law. They have abolished the free system of our laws ;
they have suspended every tribunal of justice created for
the protection of the citizen against the hand of power.
Having swept away all guarantees of personal liberty, and
property, and extended the executive power, so as to bring
every man in this great country within its grasp, they have
appealed to the legislature not only to sanction their usurpation and infidelity, but to exculpate them from criminality
and release them from responsibility for their crimes. They
have thus violated the liberty and sacrificed the property of
the citizen, and then sought to deprive him of the remedies
which are his by the rules of every civilized government.
They dare not trust their case to the judgment of the people whose cause they pretend to espouse. They violate the
law, and then try themselves upon their own indictment.
They impeach themselves of disloyalty to the Constitution
and then wipe out the offence by an act of exculpation.
This is Mr. Lincoln's government. This is the principle,
the policy and the statesmanship of anti-slavery ! This is
the Opinion which the American people have adopted in
the place of their constitutional Union !

It is not the first time in the history of nations that an
Opinion has overthrown a government and become endowed
with the powers of State. Edmund Burke, speaking of the
French revolution, near the close of the last century, says :
" Opinions without any experimental reference to their effects, when once they take strong hold of the mind, become
the most operative of all interests, and, indeed, very often
supersede every other." This anti-slavery Opinion of the

Puritan States has been the growth of years. It had its origin in England. It was reproduced in New England. It took strong hold of the Puritan mind. It soon became a fixed political dogma. I adopt the language here of Mr. Burke, in reference to French affairs. He says: "I allude to this part of history, only, as it furnishes an instance of that species of faction *which broke the locality of public affections*, and united descriptions of citizens more strangers, than with their countrymen of different opinions." This language conveys the precise truth in regard to our affairs. I propose to show how *our* opinions have effected the overthrow of the Union.

We established a purely political government. Its powers embrace only specified political interests. The moral interests of society, embracing education, police, all the domestic concerns of the people; all municipal regulations; all social government, appertain exclusively to the States. Slavery is one of these interests. It exists by virtue of no law. It is not a municipal institution, because its tenures have no affirmative legislative foundation. The people tacitly and prescriptively recognize the right of certain persons to have and enjoy the labor of negroes. This right is precisely the same as that of persons in a free State, to all personal property. It is the subject of legislation only so far as is necessary to adjust conflicting claims of individuals to it. Slavery existed in twelve of the original thirteen States. It had the same origin and *status* in all. It was not created by the statute law of either. Its abolition was a municipal regulation. Slavery was the normal condition of American society. It might exist everywhere, unless prohibited by affirmative State legislation. The late Mr. Justice Story, of the Supreme Court, speaking of the fugitive clause of the Constitution, says it was adopted "to secure to the citizens of the United States the complete right and title of ownership of their slaves, *as property*, in any State in the Union into which they might escape from the State where they were held in servitude." He adds: "The full recognition of this right and title was indispensable to the security of *this species of property* in all the slaveholding States; and, indeed, was so vital to the preservation of the domestic interests and institutions that it cannot be doubted that it constituted a *fundamental* article, without the adoption of which, the Union could *not have been formed*." This doctrine met the express concurrence of all the judges. In regard to the *status* of slavery in the Union, it is final. These views, in connection with the fact that slavery is the normal condition of our society—is a prescriptive institution, and not municipal—make it perfectly conclusive that its distinct recognition constituted, in the words of Mr. Story,

a fundamental principle of the Union. That it was regarded as a prescriptive institution of society, and received
as such by the States and the people, is proven by the fact
that it continued to exist in the District of Columbia after
its cession by Maryland and Virginia to the Federal government. Neither of those States had, by law, ordained
slavery. The adoption of their laws by Congress, in behalf of the District, after its cession to the United States,
did not affect, in any manner, the right of the people to
hold slaves. It was prescription or custom which established that right. The emancipation of all slaves, in the
District, in April last, on the other hand, prohibited slavery
--proscribed the custom under which slavery existed. So
it has been in all the States where it has been abolished.
The prescriptive interests of every community embrace quite
all the concerns of society. The State assumes the right to
regulate or abolish them on moral, religious or economical
grounds. In this category we may name ardent spirits,
indecent pictures, gaming, the protection of animals, birds,
fish and numerous other interests.

With these general principles before the reader he will
be able, the better, to appreciate the grand process of abolition in the United States, and the revolution it has effected
in the government of the Union. It is a question of cause
and effect. It is common to say, that the election of Mr.
Lincoln, in itself, was justly offensive to the slave States.
As the stone that caps the column completes the structure,
so the election of Mr. Lincoln did unquestionably finish the
work of treason to the government. By itself it was
nothing; as it organized and consolidated the opinion upon
which he was elected, it was everything. It was a most
grave event in our history ; because it armed a great family
of incendiaries and put torches in their hands with which
to murder the people and fire their homes. It made a mob
of a great nation of industrious, honest, frugal and happy
people. It filled their minds with ambition, their hearts
with malice, and their hands with plunder. It is said, I
know, that the South seceded from the Union and first
turned its armies upon our people. The historian will not
confound immediate with remote causes; he will not permit
the *last* mistake to cover all its antecedents. That is the
popular philosophy which lives and flourishes only so long as
popular passions prevail. It is the philosophy of passion.
The last mistake was, in my judgment, the inopportune secession of the South. In the movement of States the violation of the laws of discretion, from whatever motive, is
a high crime. A political blunder, involving hasty action,
though the cause may be ever so good, is a high crime.
The South was not ready for Counter Revolution. She

was without arms, ammunition, or means of defence. She had not exhausted *all* efforts at conciliation and compromise. She did not appreciate the solid friendship of great numbers—millions I may say—of the Northern people. Secession at the time, then, was a blunder—a great crime.

The first grand pervading, persistent, and criminal mistake, was the agitation of the slavery question. I apply to the latter the mildest terms. We see in it a continued effort to subvert this government, growing in magnitude, in power, in energy and bitterness, through forty years of our history. It was organized, in fact, by the Missouri Compromise, which was an act of Congress, creating a distinctive *political* North, and a political South. It created, by this process, *two* governments, under the same organic law, prohibiting in *one* what was permitted in the *other*, thus ordaining a positive inequality, in political rights, between citizens of the same common country. If Congress possessed constitutional authority to enact such a law, the policy of the act was utterly indefensible, because, at best, it proposed the compromise of a moral question, by dividing it in the centre, as one would divide an orange, without the remotest reference to practical remedies for the moral evil involved, if it existed. Judged by the lights of subsequent events, it is made perfectly clear, that while the ostensible object of the enemies of slavery, in the Missouri legislation, was to limit its extension, the real object was to inaugurate the principle that Congress had the power to control it. The successful issue of that struggle brought the whole question before the nation. It was opened at once in every Congressional District. It pervaded all society. The issue between the two interests was completely nationalized. Abolitionism at last became thoroughly organized, on the one hand, as slavery was organized on the other. That was the beginning of the end. It measured the ground and prepared the duelists for the fight. The *two* parties, thus created by act of Congress, went to work to strengthen their positions and sharpen their weapons. The aggressive power was anti-slavery, because slavery was the normal condition of all the States, as anti-slavery was the municipal condition of the free States. The North, thus relieved by act of Congress, from the comities of the Union, and established upon an independent, free territory ; a territory no longer the common property of all the States, but devoted exclusively to the free States, as was expected, at once planted itself upon an independent anti-slavery basis. The roads being all opened to the national legislature, the North saw that, by virtue of its majorities, in spite of the check which the organization of the Senate interposed, it would be able, in

a little time, to overwhelm and degrade the minorities of
the slave States. The scheme was as profound as it was
subtle and ingenious. It proposed the subversion of the
Union by the votes of the people of the free States, that
the people of the North should be educated into treason to
the Constitution—that their very habits of thought, all
moral precepts, all religious teachings—all popular con-
ceptions of right and wrong, should be turned against the
Union. As slavery was recognized by the Constitution, so
that compact must be destroyed. As the liberty of the
white race found its only exemplification in the institutions of this country, so must these be sacrificed and destroyed. As slavery was hedged in behind the government
of the Union, and the liberty of man was centered in the
American system, it became necessary, as a means to
an end, that all should be offered up on the altar of anti-
slavery. That was the sacrifice which the people were called
upon to make in order to free the enslaved Africans. Nor,
if we admit the premises of the fanatics, are they illogical.
They deny the right of man to hold man in bondage. The
corollary of the proposition follows, it is the duty of every
human being, in or out of bondage, to aid, to the extent of
his means, to destroy slavery. It is not a mere trespass, in
this sense, but a violation of God's laws affecting soul and
body. Under this inexorable logic, if to free the four million slaves of this country, it should require the death of
twenty-five million whites, it must be done.

The fight was not then urged against slavery alone, it
was waged against the Union and the States; against the
entire structure of American society. It was waged against
our very patriotism; against all received convictions of
duty; against our social and religious institutions. The
early sundering of the Methodist Church was its first great
triumph. Less successful with other religious organiza-
tions, they succeeded, nevertheless, with all, excepting perhaps the Catholics and Episcopalians, in sowing the seeds
of disunion—in destroying the oneness of their labors.
These triumphs, though not directly assailing the integrity
of the government, struck at the very root of the system.
It was a government of laws, of constitutions, of covenants;
and by its theory and practice, the people were made the
arbitors thereof. Hence every event which separated the
people of the two regions was *pro tanto* a dissolution of the
Union. The Missouri Compromise not only separated them,
but created boundaries for them. It organized them. It
vitalized and consolidated abolitionism as an aggressive
power. It opened to it a field for its labors. It gave effect
to majorities in their assaults upon the Constitution. It
destroyed the powers of minorities. It was dissolution. It

broke the religious ties which bound together the greatest evangelical society in America. It made a religion for the North and a religion for the South—morals for the North and morals for the South—a Saviour for the North and a Saviour for the South! Was this not dissolution, disruption, and antagonism? Were our political bonds strong enough to resist the power of the pulpit, the press, and the demagogue? Three thousand clergymen hurled anathemas at the late Senator Douglas for denying the constitutional jurisdiction of Congress over the subject of slavery! Ten thousand clergymen, addressing audiences numbering probably three millions of men, denounced slavery, and called down the vengeance of Heaven upon it. Was this not disunion? Did such acts strengthen the bonds of fraternity and good neighborhood, between the North and the South? Could the covenants of the Constitution be enforced under such teachings? Is it any wonder that the mob became superior to the obligations of law and the force of duty? That the mob should supersede both? That patriotism and integrity in the public councils, that fidelity in the executive office, that honesty in the citizen, should, under such circumstances, give way to disloyalty, infidelity and plunder? Justice was the power that made the Union; could it be maintained by injustice, fraud, and oppression?

It is not to be disguised that the cause of abolition has, for more than ten years, been superior to the men of the Northern States. It had gained a wonderful influence and power by the continued ascendency of the old democratic party. That party never, as an organization, yielded to it the least countenance, either in or out of the government. It denounced the prevalence of its doctrines as incompatible with the covenants of the Constitution. It declared them essential disunion. It resisted their adoption with all its influence. The opposition to the democratic party at length, in 1854, under the direct leadership of Mr. Seward, adopted a purely anti-slavery platform, and enlisted the remnants of every faction of the Northern mind in its service. The occasion for this new organization was found in the formal repeal of the Missouri Compromise, by what is known as the Kansas-Nebraska bill, of the late Senator Douglas; an act which afforded a pretext for renewed agitation of the slavery question. There was nothing in the repeal itself, because the compromise acts of 1850 had, to all intents and purposes, annulled the compromise of 1820. It was denounced, nevertheless, as the sacrifice of freedom to slavery; and thousands of ignorant and excitable people, of the free States, believed the North was about to be invaded, and, unless prompt resistance was made, conquered by the advocates of slavery! Mr. Seward,

in a speech at Columbus, Ohio, warned the people of that
State of a deliberate purpose, on the part of the South, to
invade and conquer Ohio and the entire North, including
Canada. This may seem to be exaggeration on my part,
but it is literally true. The North believed it, as much as
the assertion may reflect on its intelligence and good sense.
The Slavery campaign, it was declared, was opened by
the Kansas-Nebraska legislation; that Kansas was about
to be invaded and subdued to slavery; and that, thus
finding a base for operations, it would be continued over
the entire North, and into her Britanic Majesty's posses-
sions in Canada. This was not a mere accidental extrava-
gance of utterance by an excited political orator. It was
the deliberate speech of the first anti-slavery man of this
country. If Mr. Seward did not himself believe in the
truth of his own declarations, he certainly intended that
his audience, who heard him, and his countrymen, who
were sure to read what he said, should believe them. They
did believe them; they did more; they acted on them—
they acted on them as a declaration of war by the slavery
of the South against the freedom of the North. It was
thus that abolitionism became a political dogma. It then
assumed the attitude and the menace of a hostile party.
It made war upon slavery—it made war upon the Constitution which protected slavery, as a covenant with hell—
as a compact with the Devil. It was the people of the
North that waged this war. The State governments in
their hands, they set to work to annul the constitutional
covenant for the surrender of fugitive slaves. They denounced it as treason to enforce it. They stimulated mobs
to resist it. The mob, as I have said, thus became the
government. The South were every where denounced as
steeped in the moral guilt of slavery. Northern pulpits
were closed to the ministrations of Southern clergymen.
The negro was deified; the white man was his oppressor,
his enemy, and the enemy of humanity! Was this not
an opinion capable, when thus armed, of destroying the
Union? Could the two parties exist under the same government? If there was a moral and religious gulf between
them, which made it sacrilege to lend the sacred altars of
Christianity in the North, to the ministers of the South,
was it possible that the two peoples could maintain friendly
political relations with each other? Was not the inference
of the Southern mind, under such circumstances, inevitable,
that the North desired to sunder the political ties that
bound them to the South? Did not those ties practically
cease, when the North refused to carry out the covenants of
the Constitution?

I am perfectly aware of the principle that governments

should not be altered, modified or changed, for light or transient causes ; that mere verbal criticisms upon the institutions of the people, here or there, are not sufficient to justify such change, much less to warrant hostile revolution. I would go farther, and maintain, that none but the most insufferable evils, involving the grossest injustice and bad faith, can justify a resort to arms for the purposes of revolution. The public mind of every people is proverbially fickle and unreliable. That which is denounced to-day, is apt to be applauded to-morrow. But the revolution, in this case, commenced and was consummated in the North. The onus of its defense rests upon the North. It tore down the old system. It left not a vestige, not a remnant of its former proportions and beauty. It substituted abuse and vilification for harmony and good neighborhood. It created new systems of morals, and new articles of religious faith, for the respective regions. It dissolved quite all the social ties that bound the parties together. The federal capital witnessed the existence of a social, a religious and a political North, and a social, religious and political South. The lines were as distinct as the streets and avenues of the City. It was impossible to conceal the movements of the hostile parties. Was this not disunion and disintegration ? Could the forms of the government be maintained when its spirit had been extinguished by hatred, contempt and malice ? The North had not only refused to execute its constitutional obligations for the surrender of fugitive slaves, but the States, by their legislation, had stamped upon the covenant the seal of condemnation. This action did not alone involve the forfeiture and sacrifice of faith ; but it was so performed as to convey a gross insult to the Slave States. The Constitution was declared to be a wicked covenant which no good man could lend his aid to enforce, and which none but evil-minded men would seek to have enforced. Every effort to secure the rights of slaveholders under it, was denounced as a violation of the laws of humanity, of conscience and of justice. The power to resist was in the people of the free States; and there was scarcely a pulpit, a stage or school house, in all New England, that did not fulminate curses and imprecations against the man who would not resist the enforcement of this law of the Union. The effort too was to mark the refusal, by such acts of insubordination, as would seal forever the fate of the covenant. This was not secession; it was revolution; it was revolution inaugurated and consummated, by the strong against the weak—by majorities against minorities. It was revolution, because, at the time, the federal authorities, at Washington, and in the States, sought in

good faith, to enforce the constitutional rights of the
citizen. It was revolution by States, the parties to the
compact which they violated, and which they alone, in a
technical sense, could violate. It was gross, offensive
revolution; because it was accompanied by insulting pre-
tensions of superior morality, by the party which violated
the law! The free States thus assailed the government of
the Union in the double capacity of rebels and teachers.
It was the mob and the minister—the thief and the
apostle—the robber and the magistrate! The South, like
Paul the Apostle, were destined, it would seem, to suffer
most at the hands of their own friends—"by perils, by false
brethren." They trusted but to be deceived.

As a mere business partnership between the two regions,
the North had appropriated three-fourths of its profits,
during the entire existence of the concern. An equal propor-
tion of its dependants and employees resided in the North.
The business of the house was done in the North. It was a
Northern concern in its persons, in its profits, and in its
direction. Its revenues were nearly all derived from duties
levied upon imports. These duties were laid with a direct
view of protecting New England Manufacturers. They
gave the latter the monopoly of the American markets, by
imposing a tax upon all the manufactures and products of
other countries. They said to the people, "you shall not
buy your goods in the cheapest market, nor sell them in
the dearest. You shall buy of New England, though you
may have to pay thirty, forty or fifty per centum higher
rates than like articles could be furnished you by England
or France. We will adjust a scale of duties so as to pro-
hibit, to a certain extent, the importation of such articles
as are manufactured by New England." This was done
on the plea that our manufacturing establishments ought
to be protected by this kind of discriminating duties. It
was said they must have protection—that is, the great
agricultural labor of the West, and the South must be
taxed for the benefit of New England. That labor was
the consumer, and the consumer pays quite all the duties
collected under discriminating tariffs.

Thus it was with our business Union. Its direction, its
economical arrangements, its employees, everything that
makes money—everything that gives preponderance to
money—everything that looks to profits—were concentrated in the North. The supplies of the government were
obtained there. Its arms and implements were made there.
Its ships were built there. Its commerce was centered
there. Its laws were made there. The North has absolutely
controlled the entire economical policy of the Union for
more than forty years. Three-fourths of all the advantages

accruing to individuals under this policy, have fallen to the commercial and manufacturing States of the North. Three-fourths of all the taxes imposed upon the people to maintain the government, have been paid by the West and South.

A reference to these features of the system may seem invidious and uncalled for, at times like the present. They may seem insignificant when the government is expending two or three millions a day, to destroy the institutions under which the West and South have been taxed to the extent only of fifty or sixty millions a year, for the benefit of New England manufacturers and New York commerce. I allude to them not in the spirit of complaint, not to point even to the inequality of burdens and advantages under the old system, but to show that the disunion party—the real disunion party of the country—the Simon Pure rebels against the Union,—are those who.enjoyed quite all the material benefits which the economical administration of the government imparted. Their rebellion then must be attributed to a fretful, dissatisfied, complaining nature—to a rebellious nature,—that is the word.

Every intelligent observer of the New England mind must have been struck with the superlative estimate which the people of that uneasy corner of the Union uniformly make of themselves. Their religion is always the purest, their morals the most rigid, their schools and colleges the best ; their lawyers the ablest ; their legislators the most eloquent and profound ; their doctors the most skillful ; their teachers, their merchants, their mechanics, their artists, a little better than any other. Nature, one would think, had stamped upon the New England mind nothing but superlative degrees, being careful to advise her people of its generous dispensation. The remarkable feature of New England society is found in the fact that they know perfectly well every one of their merits, and every one of the faults and short-comings of other communities. A country that could adopt the vagaries of witchcraft, the follies of anti-Masonry, the proscriptions and injustice of Know-Nothingism, and the inhumanity of the foreign slave trade, could not be relied upon to discharge the obligations of the Constitution and perform the duties of citizens of a common government, with others. It is not treachery alone that violates the laws of a country. It is not inherent infidelity to trusts, and irresistible tendencies to forfeit the public faith, which are most offensive in the New England mind. It is an insufferable arrogance—insatiable ambition for leadership ; an ungovernable fanaticism. Their society is wanting in tone, in magnanimity, charity and in all the Christian virtues. Its grand defect, as a society, is an absence of logical power—an absence of positive philosophy

Self-opiniated and self-adulated—with eyes always in-
troverted—their premises are never well taken; their
conclusions are always false. Never losing sight of
the main chance, they have contrived, so far, to secure
quite all the benefits and advantages of the Union, and to
be the authors and propagators of quite all the heresies
which have disturbed its tranquility. And when that
tranquility is broken, it is New England that wins the
lion's share of government supplies. The present war,
instead of disturbing the labor and capital of the Puritan
States, has added to the profits of the one, and to the accu-
mulations of the other. They are actually being enriched
by what must certainly bankrupt every other region of the
country. The West and South, through the economical
policy of the Union, have contributed their money to build
up the manufacturing interests of the Eastern States, and
now, when the latter have subverted that Union and brought
the parties into civil war, they are making colossal fortunes
out of the disaster. The house has been fired to give employment and profits to the thief and the robber!

This species of political incendiarism is not a mere erup-
tive feature of the Puritan mind. It is inherent, constitutional, hereditary Fanaticism. Wise it may be, sagacious
it is; but it is the wisdom of fanaticism; the sagacity of
cunning, of policy, of management. It is that kind of cunning which discerns the advantages and benefits of strife,
contention and discord. New England has been the great
beneficiary of the Union. It is impossible, I admit, to
adjust a system of government, over large territories and
diversified interests, so as to secure a perfect equality of
burdens upon all the parts. Ours was no exception. We
made it as perfect as justice and wisdom could devise. It
was not, however, as perfect in administration as in theory
—not as pure in practice as in law. It was based on
the representative principle. This principle introduced
into it, from very necessity, advocates of peculiar interests.
Nobody questions the right of the representatives of New
England to obtain all the advantages possible for that section. The theory upon which they acted is found in the
character of the people in whose behalf they labored.
With a population five hundred thousand less than the
State of New York, they have twelve members of the Senate,
almost one-fifth of the body. They had power as well as
disposition to secure peculiar advantages. They fixed the
economical policy of the Union. They arranged the details
of that policy so as to turn quite all its incidental and positive advantages upon themselves. Had the government
been all their own, they could not have done more for themselves and less for others. Having thus essentially made the

government, they undertook in very wantonness to destroy it. Their meddling fanaticism has literally turned back upon themselves. They have destroyed forever that which alone raised them to prosperity and happiness. No matter what may be the end of the present controversy; its leveling process cannot fail to take away from New England the power she has enjoyed, of taxing the industry of other portions of the country. She piteously protested, for more than forty years, against being thrown into competition with the pauper labor of Europe. She told us of her inability, without a total overthrow of her great manufacturing establishments, to compete with that labor under free trade laws. We then proscribed free trade for her benefit, and made her the great beneficiary of the Union, whose bounty we extended to her. The money of the South and West has been paid to her labor and her capital. We adopted a system of odious discriminations to effect this. We taxed wool fabrics at high rates for her benefit; and admitted the raw material, of foreign growth, at nominal rates, for the same object. We have thus introduced foreign wool to compete with our agricultural labor and given it to New England manufacturers to be worked up and sold back to our own people under protective laws. This kind of discrimination and class legislation, said to the Puritan States: "*You* may buy in the cheapest market and sell in the dearest market,"—and to the agricultural States, " you shall *not* buy in the cheapest market nor sell in the dearest."

These things are the legitimate subject of controversy, for the purpose of showing, that no measure of advantage in the government, could hold that meddlesome people to their constitutional covenants. Had it been a question of interest, they had a motive for honesty—an inducement for maintaining the Union. It is thus seen that neither principle, advantage, patriotism, nor the memories and dignities of nationality, could control them. They clamored against the government till they destroyed it. For more than ten years they have not been members of the Union, except to reap its rewards, receive its bounties, and undermine its Constitution and laws. This rebellion is *their* rebellion—this war is *their* war. It has no other foundation, no other purpose; and can have no other end, so long as they wield the power, than to force the abolition of slavery. It is a war to enforce New England abolitionism. It is waged against the North, in its effects, more than against the South ; for the North was a greater slaveholder than the South : employed more capital, more men, and was more dependant for its prosperity upon slave labor, than the South. More than half of its foreign and domestic commerce was the direct growth of that labor. Out of three

hundred and sixty millions of exports, exclusive of the
precious metals, in 1860, two hundred and forty of them
was the product of slave labor. It was Northern capital that
conducted this enormous business. It was Northern ships
that carried those products, Northern merchants that
bought and sold them, and Northern manufacturers that
supplied the labor that raised them. The capital of
the South was almost exclusively invested in the hands that
worked their estates. The political economist will tell us, that
it is the union of labor and capital, which produces wealth ;
and that, under every known combination of this nature,
capital draws the lion's share. So it has been under the
union of Northern money with Southern labor. This rebellion strikes a fatal blow at that capital. It destroys the
most profitable and the most beneficent scheme of labor ever
devised by man. It is the work of the Puritan States against
the agricultural States of the Middle, West and South.

This view of the subject only includes the mediate interests of the Northern people with Southern slavery. It
may be said to represent the money of the North. It does
not embrace the labor of the North, which is directly employed in producing fabrics, for which the South supply
the raw material. The extent of this employment is well
understood in the rebel States of New England, where its
benefits have been quite all realized. The sudden with-
drawal of this labor, though it has seriously affected the
capital employed in it, has, so far in the war, not been felt ;
as the turn of events lodged the government exclusively
in the hands of New England men, who have commanded
the markets which the war has created. An expenditure
of two millions of dollars a day, in addition to the vast
original outlay, for implements, machinery, vessels, and
clothing, the greatest share of which the Puritan States
were called upon to supply, is quite sufficient to compensate the labor of those States heretofore engaged in the
production of cotton fabrics. The influence of this vast
engine of corruption and fraud, wielded by the hand of
absolute power, and hedged in behind the usurped authority
of a venal Congress, was more than sufficient to arm and
consolidate Abolitionism against the Constitution, and more
than sufficient to popularize the naked military despotism
conceived by that hell-begotten conspiracy—a conspiracy
which has not only overthrown the Union, but has succeeded in fastening upon its real friends, the responsibility
of the act. This last turn of events was, perhaps, to be
expected. It bears the stamp of cunning, for which the
managers of the game have been distinguished. It is not
the first time in the history of crime that the culprit has
raised the Hue and Cry, and aroused the populace in pur-

suit of his victim. It is not the first time that the thief has hidden himself and concealed his booty in the crowd of pursuers of an imaginary criminal. The great criminal of the present war is the Puritan States; its victims are the Middle, Western, and Southern States. The two former are fighting against themselves; they are fighting shoulder to shoulder with their betrayer and destroyer. They are fighting against the Union, against their interests, against their obligations, against their honor, and, as they will see within a twelvemonth, against the conscience of their people. They are fighting to put down the Constitution, to destroy their industry, to disintegrate their society, to demoralize their people, and to degrade their nationalities. Under whose direction, by whose counsel and advice, is this terrible suicide enacted?

I will name the inquisition. It is Horace Greeley, Abraham Lincoln, William H. Seward, Charles Sumner, Wade, of Ohio, Wilson, of Massachusetts, Trumbull, of Illinois, Chase, of Ohio, Garrison, Phillips, Beecher, and Cheever. These are the twelve apostles of infidelity and crime—the Satanic Council—who have been chosen to enforce this infernal atonement of blood—this reconciliation of slaughter! They call it a remedy! They say it is a patriotic impulse! It is a substitute for all that is good in free institutions, for all that is reputable in our national character, and for all that is successful and honorable in civil society.

This brings me to state what occurs to me to be the only legal remedy for popular diseases, under our constitutional government. It is the ballot. The ballot is the organ of speech of this nation. It had the power to correct any and every abuse of its authority. It had jurisdiction over secession; even secession in the Puritan States. It could restore order in the midst of revolution. The directing power over everything was in the people. All they wanted was time and opportunity, to speak. This could be done through the ballot only under prescribed forms. In the midst of the pending crisis, it was proposed by Mr. Crittenden and others, in Congress, to arm the ballot instead of the people—to give it authority to direct and determine the differences between the North and South. Every republican voted against it. The South at first hesitated; but at length, through its organs, endorsed it. It was the remedy of peace. That was what the South wanted; that was just what abolitionism would not, under any circumstances, have. The ballot would maintain the Constitution, and, by maintaining it, uphold slavery and the rights of slaveholders; that was what abolitionism would not have. The ballot would settle and adjust all our differences; that was what would kill abolitionism. Peace preserves and

strengthens a people; that was what abolitionism most
feared. The North must be armed—her majorities must
be armed; because they were majorities, and because the
South was disarmed. They vainly thought arms, to be
effective, must be in the hands; they never for once
thought that arms in the head and heart are more terrible.
They saw nothing but numbers, money, and credit; they
did not see that all these have a substitute in resolution,
conviction, and duty. "Thrice is he armed who hath his
quarrel just." But it was abolitionism, so they thought,
that could invoke the truth of this philosophical maxim.
They were fighting against oppression—they were fighting
against the Union as a mob in the way of the enforcement
of their higher law—their abolitionism. Was this not the
theory of the Satanic Council? Why else did they arm
against the South, and disarm and imprison the protestants
of the North? Why else did they sweep away, as with a
broom, the rights and guarantees even of the people of the
free States? Why else, in a word, did they cancel, by a
single executive blow, the Constitutional Government of
the Union? Is it common to destroy what one would im-
prove and purify? to kill what we wish to cure and preserve? Did their hostility to the South conceal real devotion and friendship to the old system? Did policy pilot their
principles, and shelter and conceal their patriotic designs?
    The answer to these questions is found in the record of
violated rights and executive usurpations. It is found in
the fell spirit of abolitionism, which pervades and controls
every act of the administration, and every movement of the
army. It is found in the adoption of its schemes of violence
and fraud everywhere, and the exclusion of every measure
calculated to stop the war and harmonize the belligerents.
If the people are so struck with judicial blindness that they
are unable to comprehend these things, their welfare has
engrossed too much thought and anxiety. If they are
willing not only to be grossly deceived and misled, but
made pack-horses and sumpter-mules for thieves and rob-
bers, I do not perceive the difference, in moral guilt,
between them and the original Puritan culprits.
    But it is said the South commenced the war. That the
men of the South opened their batteries upon the men of
the North, I admit. That they inaugurated actual war, I
also admit. I think it was a great political blunder, and
therefore a crime; that it was without cause, or in opposition to the principles of the Federal Government, I deny.
The South made war against the new government—against
the new system,—in behalf of the old government, and in
defence of the old system. It was a war waged against
the revolutionary government of New England, in defence

of the rights of minorities. It was undertaken only when the powers of the Constitutional Union were confessedly used to disfranchise and destroy those minorities. It was a mistake only in being out of time, and in using, for the moment, the wrong remedy. It was called by a bad name, and its name gave it an illogical character. The South said they had a *right*, as Sovereign States, to secede from the Union. That was an error—a damaging error, for in reality they had no such right. Secession was a New England remedy and practice, and never should have been invoked. It is a mischievous, if not an absurd theory. The *right* of secession could not have been *reserved* without imparting to the Union an external character, at war with the policy of the nation. All governments are supposed to be perpetual. A government gains first, recognition, and then commands respect by virtue of the evidence it is able to exhibit to the world, of its ability to preserve its organism and perpetuate its power. Perpetuity is a vital element of its character. Besides, there would be no force whatever, in a covenant, express or implied, reserving the right of secession ; because, no member of the Union could ever avail itself of such a right, except *for good cause,* and where the latter exists, it could not be strengthened by any reservation in the bond—in other words, no State could justify itself for secession, simply, because it had the *right* to secede. Such a reservation would have no force, whatever. 1. Because it would be incompatible with the policy of the nation. 2. Because it would not be even *prima facia* evidence that the act was right. A promissory note is prima facia evidence of indebtedness : but this presumption may be rebutted by proof of payment, so that the case is made to turn after all upon its merits. The rule of law, however, governing notes and bills of exchange, made for the benefit and convenience of trade, is hardly applicable to constitutions of government. The latter embody fundamental principles which are supposed to be irrepealable and indestructible. This is their character in all cases. When grossly violated, the *legitimate* remedy is revolution. There is dignity in the word, and gallantry, spirit and resolution in the act. Revolutions refer, properly, to causes. God is the sovereign arbiter of causes, as man is the arbiter of covenants. The Puritan States overturned the government of the Union, and installed in its place a mob. No allegiance was actually due to that mob from anybody. It was a mob, because when they destroyed the old system, they left no legitimate power, except the States, to govern. They wielded, it is true, the powers of the Union ; but they wielded them not in obedience to, but in contempt of the

Federal Constitution. The South warred against this mob.
They wanted the old system; and they blundered that
they ever gave up the name of the old system. There is
little in a name, it is said; there was much under the circumstances, in the name of the old government; because
by using it, the rebels of New England could the more
certainly mislead the popular mind, and put the constitu-
tionalists of the South in the wrong. They were not, I
maintain, altogether in the right upon the main question.
It does not often happen that great matters of difference
between nations are so exquisitely balanced as to have the
right all on one side, and the wrong all on the other. The
question of slavery in the territories was invoked by the
North as an instrumentality, not as a measure or principle.
Abolitionism, it is seen, from the very nature of its
theories, and the ends it proposed to accomplish, cared
nothing for mere territorial slavery. The territories, lost
or won, were nothing to them. They raised the point to
act *from*, not to act *upon*. They *used* the territorial dispute
as an agency through which to excite and inflame the
people against slavery in the States. As early as 1841,
they became convinced that they could never succeed in
consolidating the North against the Union, so long as
they suffered themselves to be identified with a party
having a pro-slavery wing. Hence the rupture with the
old whig party, and the adoption of a programme which
made it impossible to extend their lines into the slave
States. The present Secretary of the Treasury was a leader
in this work of Independent Abolitionism — Northern
abolitionism—New England abolitionism. In 1843 he
was a member of a convention at Buffalo, New York,
which resolved to "regard and treat the third clause of
the Constitution, whenever applied to the case of a fugitive
slave, as utterly *null* and *void, and, consequently, as forming
no part* of the Constitution of the United States, *whenever
we are called upon or sworn to support it.*" Afterwards Mr.
Butler, of South Carolina, denounced this infamous act of
secession, miscalling it a system of mental reservations.
There was no mental reservation in it; it was downright
nullification and subornation of perjury. It was an open,
flagrant declaration of war against the federal Constitution.
In 1854 the present republican, or abolition, party was formally organized, with Mr. Seward at its head. It was
then believed to be strong enough to wield Northern
majorities against the Union; to give practical effect to its
resolutions of previous years, to nullify and make void
the Constitution, and ordain an anti-slavery government.
Its power, in this way, to destroy the old system, no man
of sense and observation could question; and that the

scheme of wielding majorities against the constitutional rights of the States and the people, would effect this, was equally certain. The organization of the Union was accomplished with a direct and express view of protecting minorities. To this end it was ordained that the weakest State should have a representation in the federal Senate equal to the largest; that none other than expressly delegated powers should be exercised; that all others should be reserved "to the States respectively, or to the people." The great doctrine of the Union was the protection of minorities. This principle of the system was assailed by the organization of the abolition party. That party said, "hereafter, majorities shall be supreme." This was not secession, it was revolution; it was complete, absolute revolution. This principle was first applied to the territories, as the wedge is first inserted into the timber it is destined subsequently to rend asunder. The South resisted it, and made more of it than the merits of the question authorized. They resisted it more on account of the insult it covered, than the real sacrifice of rights it threatened. Territorial slavery, in every political sense, was a pure abstraction. The law of climate and soil had settled it. There was not a foot of really disputed ground. If, under other circumstances, there had been any doubt upon this point, there was another law that had determined the matter beyond all question. Slavery is a relation of interest, as indicated by its profit and loss account. The most profitable fields for its labor were in the slave States, and they were broad enough not only to employ the four million slaves now held, but quite four times that number. There could then be no expansive power, in slavery, beyond the limits of the States where it existed. Just as men seek the highest markets for the sale of their produce, so will slaveholders seek the most profitable field for their labor. It was not, then, the slave interests, but the political interests of the South that were menaced by the territorial policy of the abolitionists. It was not slavery that was the object of direct assault, but the constitutional government of the Union. That must be stricken down, and removed, as an obstacle in the way of general emancipation. It was a covert attack, made as much against the North as against the South. It was the substitution of the Opinions of New England, in the place of the covenants of the Union. The power that impelled this engine of destruction was that Opinion. It was proclaimed from every pulpit; it was inculcated at every fireside, and taught in every school-house and college of the Puritan States. The walls of those houses and colleges, in many parts of the country, displayed, in bill-head letters, these

insulting words: "Slavery is the unpardonable sin!"
Nor were there any deceptions practised upon the people
in these teachings and utterances. They proclaimed an
exterminating war against the Constitution. They denounced it as a league with Satan, and declared allegiance
to it incompatible with the exercise of Christian duties,
thus making the government an unbearable moral nui-
sance, which it was God's service to abate.

It is not my purpose to exaggerate this picture of
Puritan infidelity and enmity to the Union, and the domestic institutions of the South. I do not think it in the
power of any man to do this, having regard to justice and
truth. That enmity was all that abuse of men, treachery
to principles, infidelity to covenants, and inborn fanaticism,
could make it. It was as cunning as it was malignant and
unfaithful. It had no easy work to accomplish. A skillful
hand must always be at the helm to guide the pirate crew
between Scylla and Charybdis. To wield too much power
would alarm the people ; to wield too little would render
them unattractive, if not insignificant. The weapon of
warfare chosen—that of majorities—was, of all others, the
best and most effective. There is a charm in majorities ;
the people think they are the directing power ; they cannot see why it is not right that the majority should
govern ; and they feel that it is the duty of the minority
to submit. This is the logic of the mob—it is the logic of
the New England rebellion. When this doctrine became
the government, in the inauguration of Mr. Lincoln, how
did the propagandists demean themselves towards the
government of the Union, and the people of the South?
Were they faithful to the covenants of the one, and to the
rights of the other? If the Slave States had been prejudged
and condemned, what was their conduct towards the people
of the free States—towards the minorities of the free States?

One of the first acts of Mr. Lincoln was to suspend the
functions of the judiciary. Nothing but the venerable age
and exalted character of Chief Justice Taney saved him
from arrest and imprisonment for declaring, on the bench,
that the acts of the President were unconstitutional and
void. A man who is justly the pride of the country, who
dignifies the first judicial office of the nation, was openly
branded with disloyalty to that Constitution, which Mr.
Lincoln and all his adherents openly violated at every turn !
He was denounced as a traitor, and the vengeance of the
mob invoked against his life ! And what was his offence?
An attempt to vindicate the supremacy of the laws for the
protection of a citizen of the loyal States against the arbitrary and unconstitutional acts of the President of the
United States. Faithful to the Union, he sought, by the

exercise of powers vested in him, as the head of the judicial department, to wipe out the stain of usurpation which the chief magistrate had imprinted upon the sacred folds of the Constitution. His attempt was futile. His orders were disregarded. His process could not be served. The marshal reported that he " was not permitted to enter the gate " of Fort McHenry, where a citizen was imprisoned without " process of law," and in violation of the Constitution. The reasons assigned by the venerable judge for excusing the marshal for not serving the process should be engraved upon every monument erected in honor of American patriots, statesmen and philosophers. He said :

" You had the power to summon the *posse comitatus* to aid you in seizing and bringing before the Court the party named in the attachment, who would, *when so brought in,* be liable to punishment by fine and imprisonment. But where, as in this case, *the power refusing obedience was so notoriously superior* to any you could command, I hold that you are excused from doing more than you have done."

What power was this that resisted the enforcement of the rights of a citizen ? It was the President—the power which was lodged in his hands, that he might see to it that the laws should be faithfully executed ! It was the government against itself, against the laws, against the Constitution ! It was the mob triumphant, by the aid of the President, in opposition to the laws, against John Merryman ! Whatever was left of the old system was trampled under foot by this executive act. It was more damaging to the integrity of that system than the battles of Manassas and Fredericksburg. Battles could not destroy what was destroyed by this act. Battles may suspend the powers of government, here or there ; they do not immolate principles or impair the integrity of constitutions. This conduct of the President was in harmony with the revolutionary theory under which he was elected. He acted in aid of that theory. He carried out the resolution at Buffalo, to nullify and make void " the third clause of the Constitution, whenever applied to the case of a fugitive slave ; " he enforced the nullification laws of Massachusetts, ordained to carry out that resolution ; he made the government an anti-slavery government—a New England government. His act was an act of war against the Union. The personal liberty of John Merryman, and his honored associates, in prison, was nothing. The time had come to wield power, and make it felt as a means of intimidation—to strengthen the new government—to make it absolute—to make all the people *feel* that it was absolute. The conquest of the North was as necessary as the conquest of the South. The conspirators knew that while they were elected to office

by a majority of the people of the North, the development
of their revolution would throw them back into a miserable minority. Their purpose was to arm this minority,
and, by an exercise of power, to force the entire Northern
people to submit to their revolutionary government. This
is no speculative theory, but a great historical fact. It is
sustained by every act of Mr. Lincoln's government affecting persons or principles. It is sustained by every ante-
cedent of the party which elected him. It is sustained by
the speeches of every leader of that party, in or out of
Congress, at the present day. It is sustained by the pro-
motion of Abolitionists to command the armies, and the
proscription of every Unionist, who has won military dis-
tinction in the field. It ought to be enough to prove the
justice of this theory, that the new government has created,
in the place of the old one, an absolute military despotism
—a despotism which has proscribed every guarantee of personal rights contained in the Federal Constitution ; which
has annulled or disregarded State laws ; which has created
new offences, unknown to the United States, and then, by
a sweeping decree, suspended the writ of Habeas Corpus,
as to all persons " who are now, or hereafter during the
rebellion, shall be imprisoned in any fort, camp, arsenal,
military prison or other place of confinement, *by any military authority.*" (See Proc. 24 Sept.) This final act of
despotic power was only a formality. All rights and guarantees had been previously swept away. The work of revolution had been already perfected. It only proclaimed a law
that had been in existence from the day of the President's
inauguration. Emancipation had been going on by every
general in the field, and by every paid agent of the government, who could steal, rob or plunder. The process did
not embrace alone the capture of slaves ; it proposed the
destruction of property of every description, the burning
of buildings, the waste of estates, the suffering and sacrifice of the people of the slave States, in every imaginable
form ; for, it was said, by these means we shall paralyze
slavery, and thus deprive it of the power of self-defence.

Was this not revolution ? Was it the policy of the
Union that dictated this scheme of plunder, arson and murder ? Was it not armed Abolitionism ? Could such things
occur under the old government ?

All governments are agencies. This, at least, is the
American theory. Some exist by prescription, or by
what is called Divine appointment; others by virtue of
laws ordained by the people. Prescriptive governments,
as I shall call them, are supposed, nevertheless, to represent the will and have the sanction of the masses for whom
they were created. The rights of the people under the

latter are just as sacred, and as safe, it is thought by many, as under the former. I know of no government, of this class, which does not profess to represent the will and the interests of its constituency. That of Russia, is, perhaps, the most completely absolute, in its powers, of all the States of Europe. Austria and the Imperial government of France are next in rank. Every one of these has been surpassed in despotic practice by the government of the United States. The absolutism of the latter, judged by measures, is more extreme than either of the European States referred to. There is less security here, to persons ; more arbitrary and causeless arrests and imprisonments ; more interference of the executive authority with the duties and functions of the judiciary ; more property sacrificed by persons and tribunals appointed and *created* by the President ; more government frauds; more official peculations ; and more public demoralization than in either of the great absolutistic States mentioned. That these discreditable and disastrous effects of abolitionism, are not the product of legitimate American opinions and judgment, is more than apparent ; and that they are the fruits of New England fanaticism and folly, is susceptible of the clearest proof. No calm observer of events in this country, for the last quarter of a century, can doubt the justice of this declaration. Personal ambition and selfishness, have united with the more honest but misguided followers of Garrison, Phillips and Greeley, to bring on the present crisis. The former class entered the ranks of the fanatics not because they concurred in the doctrines of abolitionism, nor yet because they really intended to effect its revolutionary ends. Their object was to *use* that school of madmen— and hence, we all remember, that for years, there was a sort of *quasi* league between the parties, wearing a very cordial aspect just before and at elections, but invariably followed by an open rupture. As between the two factions it soon became evident that the Abolitionists proper had the most votes and the most power. Those who had propagated anti-slavery, to advance their own political purposes, found they had carried over the majority to the minority. Under such circumstances it only required a Presidential election to enlist on the side of the Abolitionists every faction, interest and combination opposed to the dominant Democratic party. That a large portion of the persons thus enlisted, intended to revolutionize the government, no man believes. They contributed, nevertheless, all that votes could do to effect this. They placed men in power who had again and again declared a purpose to destroy the Union. They were guilty of a high offence in a popular government, that of aiding to elect to office persons who

had avowed doctrines at war with the political system they
desired to maintain. The conspirators, after they assumed
the reigns of government, took advantage of this known
partiality and admiration for the Union, and through its
influence drew to their support, and to their rebellious and
treasonable schemes, not only all of this class of persons,
but also a large portion of the Democratic party. These
men were perfectly sincere in the aid they gave the administration, never doubting its fidelity to the Union, and
never dreaming, for a moment, that the real enemy to the
old system was the party they had elected to its offices.
The loyal sentiment of the North, in this way, was more
thoroughly duped than the South ; because the interests of
the latter were directly menaced, and they were forced by
this menace to assume the defensive. Their secession was
inopportune ; because their votes, united to the votes of
Northern Democrats, in both Houses of Congress, were
sufficient to check and defeat the scheme of the conspirators to invest the executive head with absolute powers.
Thus, holding the administration at bay, the South, by
remaining in the Union, would have gained time to pre-
pare for the struggle, and, perhaps, ultimately defeat the
conspirators. The latter result, I believe, might have been
achieved ; but it is very questionable whether any perma-
nent adjustment was possible without a resort to arms.
The mind that directed the abolition movement was essentially deficient in logical powers. Its insolence, its tendencies to disregard obligations and duties ; its ignorance
of the character of the government, and the ends for which
it was established ; its inherent fanaticism and the presumption which these qualities could not fail to develope,
not only prove this, but made any political association with
it next to impossible. If it had exhibited no other radical
deficiency, its habitual cunning and want of integrity
were enough to destroy any union formed by human covenants. Out of power, they nullified the Constitution and
resisted the enforcement of Federal laws ; in power, they
overthrew the Constitution and established a military despotism in its place. Out of their hands, the Union was
an immoral covenant, which no man was bound to recognize ; in their hands, their despotism is a sacred compact by which minorities agree to be sacrificed by majorities. Judged by their acts, one would suppose, that the
Constitution was adopted, with no other purpose or end,
than to effect the abolition of slavery—that it is a fundamental law of a New England anti-slavery society. The
late message of the President, and every measure of
his administration, point directly to this conclusion.
That such a government never was ordained by the States ;

that it is a new government, ordained by the abolitionists, to all practical intents and purposes, must be apparent to every thinking mind. The process by which this result has been effected, I have endeavored to trace ; the responsibility of the parties to it, I have also endeavored to establish. No stream is so long, or so crooked, that its source may not be discovered ; no deception and fraud are so ingenious and intricate, that they cannot be analysed and exposed. The Union was an agreement between sovereign States, to form a Nationality, on certain specified conditions. Its enemies are those who violated those conditions. Such violation made it impossible for the honest parties to the agreement to maintain it. It was not a solid popular nationality—a concrete system—it was made of sovereign States, not by sinking them in the Union, but by maintaining them as practical governments, as the basis of the system—as the legal parties to the agreement. It is manifest in this view of the subject, that the nullification of the Constitution, by the New England States, was an act of revolution, which absolved all the other States from obligations to carry out the agreement. But an indisposition to disturb the government, with which so many great interests were identified, induced the other parties to submit, for the time, to this infraction of the organic law. But when it became obvious that such submission only invited further and more radical violations of the Constitution, and threatened its total subversion, and the employment of its powers, not only to disfranchise, but to destroy a great section of the country, resistance became a necessity and a high duty. This resistance should not have been confined to the Slave States. They were the immediate objects of assault and sacrifice ; but as these involved the forfeiture of faith, and the violation of solemn covenants, by parties to the Union, resistance became the duty of every honest man in the nation. It was not a Northern and Southern question, but a question of integrity and fair dealing; and as the North became an implicated party, it was its duty, *as a section*, to vindicate its honor by acts of prompt resistance. We have advanced too far in the science of political ethics, to maintain, in case of a violation of the covenants of offensive and defensive Treaties, between States, that the duty of resistance should be confined to the injured party. The benefits and advantages of such a compact are reciprocal, and they impose, upon the parties to it, reciprocal duties and obligations, to maintain its integrity, in the event of its infraction by either party. When the Puritan States nullified the fugitive slave clause of the Constitution, and

made it a penal offence for one of their turbulent citizens
to aid in its enforcement, it became the duty of every other
State in the Confederacy, at once, and by the most ener-
getic measures, to force the delinquents to comply with
their obligations, or leave the Union. Their failure to
do this, stamped upon the federal system an indelible
stain, which no subsequent effort could remove. It was
thus *tainted* with disloyalty, infidelity, injustice, and fraud.
It introduced into the government, and canonized, a class
of men, whose avowed purpose was to destroy it. It gave
the key to the house-breaker, and told him where the
valuables were concealed. This was revolution. No
system of government could stand such a shock. I do not
believe armed resistance was necessary ; certainly not, if
the Middle and Western States had done their duty.
They saw, or ought to have seen, that one great step
towards the overthrow of the Union—one which could
hardly fail to effect that cherished object—was to *taint*
it with injustice. This was effectually done by the Puri-
tans ; and it was accomplished without a single remon-
strance, as far as I can learn, from the free States. The
integrity of the latter was involved ; but local partisan
interests, it was feared, might be injured by the adoption
of immediate measures, and these must be taken care of,
even if the government should be sacrificed. It is vain to
deny that partisan causes, in this way, have blunted the
sensibilities, and lowered the tone of all Northern society.
That there are great numbers of individual exceptions,
embracing, in some cases, whole communities, I do not
doubt. But partisanism is, nevertheless, a sort of epi-
demic in all the Northern States. The question is, *not*
what is right, but what will be most taking with the
people. Every sail is set to the popular breeze. By this
process, demagogues and adventurers alone are promoted
to office, and give character to the State. No heresy is too
monstrous to find advocates ; no dishonesty too flagrant
to be sanctioned. It is not a question of integrity ; but
whether the proposed measure is one which has found
favor with the people. This is no exaggeration of practical
politics in the North ; and, although not applicable, to
the same extent, to the South, is more or less true, there.
It is an evil inherent in all representative or democratic
governments. More positive virtue is certainly necessary,
in such governments, than under monarchical systems.
The reason for this is found more perfectly illustrated in
the United States than elsewhere. We have armed the
demagogue with power, and made him not only our
governor, but our teacher. He is in the pulpit, at the bar,
in the school-house, in the legislature, on the bench, and

he is now President of the United States. We have
priestly demagogues, legal demagogues, judicial demagogues, and Congressional demagogues. Our Executive
Magistrate is a cross between the demagogue and the
fanatic, with a decided leaning to the former. He has been
called honest: time will prove that his cunning has been
mistaken for honesty, his plain speech, for candor, and his
blunt ways, for sincerity. He is the representative of
abolitionists and demagogues. That is all there is in him.
Too weak to devise schemes of treason against the Union,
he is admirably fitted, by his moral nature, to carry out
the programme of revolution arranged by others. When
nature denies attributes of intellect and honesty to man,
she is apt to compensate him by endowments of intrigue
and cunning. These are Mr. Lincoln's great qualities of
head and heart. No management of the elements of disunion could have been better or more successful than his.
Battles lost, for his purpose, were better than battles won.
What he wanted was protracted war and irreconcilable
differences. By no other means was it possible to over-
turn the old system, and organize a despotism in its place.
The disgraceful rout at Manassas was the grand triumph
of Abolitionism. It was equal to a half a million recruits
to his new government; it turned the heads and hearts of
ten million men against the South. Power was then
literally thrust into his hands. The people demanded that
he should wield it against themselves! Was ever anything
more opportune? Did a great people ever before determine
to disfranchise themselves, and to assure the completeness
of their work, actually build up a military despotism upon
the ruins of their ancient free institutions? The gulf is,
indeed, narrow between liberty and despotism!

Having traced, with some minuteness, and in detail, the
great Revolution inaugurated and consummated under the
auspices and management of the Puritan States, and
referred to the counter revolution of the Slave States, I
think it opportune to make a few suggestions of a hypo-
thetical nature, touching the future of the regions of the
Country, North and South. A full examination of the
past convinces me that the only ground of real difficulty
between the Free and the Slaves States is found in the turbulent and offensive nature of the Puritan mind. At the
first glance, this may be regarded as an insurmountable
obstacle in the way of fellowship between the people of the
two sections. But a moment's reflection is enough to
convince the reader that it is not so. The Puritan States
may be cut off from the confederacy without at all affecting the strength or beauty of the system. They contribute
nothing to the national character, except, possibly, what

we gain by extravagant self-laudation and praise. There
is nothing in New England which is necessary to give
strength to the Federal Government,—nothing which is
necessary to complete a confederation in any sense whatever. The Government of the Union was so conducted as
to confer upon the six small States of the East quite all
the wealth and position they have gained. They are
nothing but an extended manufacturing establishment.
We do not need such establishments. We can not much
longer, in any event, afford to keep them up. We have
enriched them by our bounties : but there must, sooner or
later, be an end of this. England is quite able to do our
mechanical work. She has a great many very poor, but
expert, mechanics. We shall be doing them and ourselves
a great service by buying their fabrics and machinery.
This kind of trade will stimulate commerce and agricul-
ture. We shall have all the benefits of low wages, without being burdened with the support of that class of society.
The construction of a government on free-trade principles,
—excluding New England, which must, sooner or later,
be done,—would go far to harmonize all disputes, and
would certainly assure the most complete and successful
industry which the world has ever seen. There is no
obstacle in the way of either reconciliation, or future harmony, if the Puritan States were removed. The great
West is yet in its infancy. It has, so far, submitted
quietly to the dictation and plunder of the New England
States. This can not last long. They will not always,
surely, consent to be taxed thirty or forty millions a year
for the benefit of what the fanatics call "domestic manufactures;" and once in a half century, at least, be saddled
with a debt of a thousand millions of dollars, to get them
out of the difficulties engendered wholly by New England.

The present complications, then, which demand a solution—which must, ere long, have a solution—ought to
indicate to the Middle and Western States that the time
is rapidly approaching when it will be their duty—just as
it is the duty of any man to resist robbery—to force the
Puritan States *to rely on themselves*. That is all the punishment one has the heart to inflict upon them. Take
away from them the peculiar advantages which the federal
system secures them. Let them live by their own labor,
in competition with the labor of others. Let them have
every advantage which the past has given them. They
have accumulated wealth : it is theirs. They have built
up great manufacturing establishments : they are theirs.
They have wonderful industry, economy, and business ca-
pacities. Give them the full benefit of these, but nothing
more. They are really too good to live in peace with the

rest of mankind! Let them set up for themselves. If they can manufacture cheaper than others, they may always be sure of a market. This can be tried only by making New England an independent confederacy. For one, I would not only rejoice to see this, but would feel most confident that the great Western and Southern States would rejoice with me. Five years' experience under such an order of things would show the benefits of the arrangement. It would enrich the great agricultural States. It would make them free. It would stimulate local manufactures. It would distribute labor. It would reduce— greatly reduce—the expenses of living. The money they would thus save in fifty years would doubly pay the present national debt. Why not, then, obey a great necessity of the future, and put New England out of the Union now? There may be danger in delay. The great West cannot, and will not, be cut off from the navigation and markets of the Mississippi. A little time, and they will turn to the South. There are no affinities between them and New England. That which *now* binds them to the East is the railway, a power kindred to that which binds them to the Valley of the Mississippi. The relations between the Puritan States and the West are that of landlord and tenant. The former own everything, and make their own terms. They compel the West to buy of them, and to pay their own prices. The Government of the United States says, "you must buy of New England; for we wish to make New England so rich that they can compete with the manufacturers of Old England." The West does not care a fig about the manufactures of either of the rival parties. She wants to buy her goods in the cheapest market; and this she will do as certain as the West is great and growing. Make New England a separate government, and the great States of the South and West will be relieved of a burden of expense, which can not fail in ten years to show *how New England got rich.*

Self-preservation is the first law of nature. It is as applicable to states as to individuals. The Government of the Union had all the advantages which it is possible to confer upon, or exist in, a State. Her system was liberal; her geographical position conducive to peace, and, in the event of war, wonderfully defensive, if not inaccessible; her climates various; her products valuable and always marketable; her Government respected, and her people prosperous and happy. There has not been one single source of real discord out of New England. If the economical policy of the Union was oppressive and unsatisfactory to the agricultural districts, the burden fell upon a liberal, uncomplaining, patriotic people, who never, except

the turbulent State of South Carolina, for a moment,
thought of disturbing the organic system, as a remedy.
The incurable malady, then, being found in a mere limb
of the body—the vital organs being sound and healthy—
why not cut it off? The application of the knife, instead
of a resort to the materia medica, is the true course;
because more than three-fourths of a century have proven
the incurability of the disease. No people,—in plain
words,—will ever be able to live in harmony with the
Puritan States. If they are wiser and better than the rest
of mankind, it is just as fatal to harmonious fellowship as
if they occupied the reverse of this position. They are
utterly unlike other people. Their tempers and dispositions are so entirely different from those of the Middle,
Western, and Southern States, as to render fellowship
with them, under the same government, impossible. The
remedy I have suggested is simple, honest, and just. It is
to *let New England alone!* Let her try her separate fortunes.
If she will quarrel, let her quarrel with New England. If
she will turn back upon herself and destroy her own works,
let us be exempt from her lunacy, while the paroxysm is on.

A confederated government in this country, being a
simple government of independent States, united for specific
general objects, cannot be maintained unless all the parties
to it strictly discharge the obligations of the compact.
Such a government will always be the strongest, or the
weakest, in the world. If there is unity of purpose, and
action, it will be invincible in respect to its aggressive and
productive powers. The effort of the parties to it should
be to exhibit generosity and fidelity in all federal relations.
Where, on the other hand, these great qualities are wanting, it is with the State, as with individuals, a sure sign
of demoralization, strife, and weakness. The Government
of the Union has existed for three-quarters of a century,
and, by maintaining its perfect integrity, might have had
a career of prosperity and greatness, not only without
parallel in the history of nations, but so successful, that,
by the force of example alone, it would, within fifty years,
have governed the world. I do not mean to assert that all
the nations would have been drawn into the Union: because that is an impossibility. They would, nevertheless,
have been influenced and controlled by its example. This
we have lost ; and it is the greatest of our losses in the
present suicidal war. It is not only a loss to us, but it is
a loss to every liberal mind throughout the world. Great
principles speak through governmental forms, far more
effectively than through individuals. They must have de-
monstration by action, to make them influential and powerful. This consideration, I humbly suggest, has been to

much overlooked by the men of both sections of the Union. They have been too much absorbed in selfishness and pride of position, to give due weight to the high interests involved in the late Government of the Union. They have overlooked the interest which liberalism everywhere had in the maintenance of that Government. I suppose such considerations as these never had the least weight with, perhaps never entered the minds of, the Puritan States. Their conduct in the Union has evinced nothing but sharp practice and dissolute political morals. The first fifty years of its existence, they worked alone to secure undue advantages ; the balance of the time they have devoted to its overthrow. So that, in every light in which their conduct is seen, they have been most unworthy associates. Their ejection from the Government, then, under the inexorable logic of events, is certain, sooner or later. The truth can not always be concealed : it will surely work its own way to light. There is too much cool reflection, too much sound sense, and too much honesty in the great body of the American people, to be held many years longer, as dupes and tools, by that meddlesome race of political sharpers and thimble-riggers. They have never contributed any thing to the people which could not have been obtained, on better terms, of others. To have something to do with every man's business, and contrive to turn it to good account, is the life of a New England man. He is a disturber and meddler by nature. He goes everywhere—talks to everybody—makes all the difficulties he can foment—and then turns everything to his own profit. This kind of character can do best by himself. Let him alone. Build up a high wall round his dominions. Confine his labors to his own territories and his own people.

PERSONAL AND POLITICAL.

The writer of these pages is a Northern man—has been a citizen, for thirty-five years, of the State of New York. With little ambition for political life, and not overburdened with confidence in the public men of the country, North and South, he has been an unprejudiced witness of all the great events, which, in his judgment, have led to the present disastrous war.   He has ever been a Unionist, not for the benefits and advantages alone, which the constitutional government assured to the two sections now at war, not because he believed the system absolutely perfect ; nor yet on account of its sacred origin, but because in the Union of the States, he thought he saw the power and the disposition to uphold free government in the very face of a world of Absolutism ; and, that if stricken down here, there would be left no hope of maintaining it elsewhere.   The Union, in this sense, was not for the American people alone; it was organized freedom for all the world.   Freedom could speak here, could act here.   It was a teacher, a producer and an exemplar.   It had power to defend itself, and propagate by example, the great principle upon which it was organized.   Entertaining these views, it was quite natural to regard with distrust, the introduction into the government of doctrines, which a large portion of the people North, and all the people South, believed would destroy it.   That Abolitionism would effectually do this, *if carried into the Government*, no man of sense could doubt.   The question was, how far it was the intention of its advocates to push the doctrine.   Many believed it was *used* only to advance personal ambition ; others were convinced that, although that might be its aim, when weak, it would, from the nature of things, be impossible to limit its action thus, when strong.   Others regarded it as pre-eminently a New England opinion, which the politicians of the Middle and Western States might *use*, always retaining the power to check and subdue it, when it should menace the integrity or stability of the government.   Others still—and as the sequel abundantly proves, they were the wise and patriotic men of the nation—regarded the rising storm, as not only threatening, but destined, in its progress, to destroy the Union.

The authenticity of the New, is established by the prophecies of the Old, Covenant.   This kind of testimony, applied to political affairs, may not be as conclusive as when invoked in behalf of christianity.   What it wants in credibility, as a mere political prophecy, is, however, more than supplied by the living testimony of men and things of the present generation.   Political predictions signify nothing more than that the human mind is able to comprehend, at a glance, the active forces of the State, and distinguish which of these will control the others in the future, and what the result will be.   This kind of foreknowledge, when recorded in advance, is high testimony, because it was so uttered, and because historical events have determined its substantial verification ; and shown that its author was an unprejudiced observer of men and things—was able to discover the motives of the one and dispositions of the other.

It required little sagacity in a citizen of this country, to foretell the doom of the republic, under the operation of the principles, which have been warring against it, with such terrible energy, especially since 1854, when the great North formally organized its forces, on the basis alone of the Abolition of Slavery. At that period, the reader will remember, we had five distinct political parties, viz : the hard democrats, the soft democrats, the whigs, the know-nothings or Natives, and the Abolitionists. The latter party made a powerful and successful effort—a purely Northern effort—to absorb them all into one grand anti-slavery organization. There was no difficulty in effecting this object, so far as the know-nothings were concerned, because that party was a mere scrofulous eruption upon the body politic, which must kill or cure in a day. Its seat was in New England, where the people were anti-union and anti-slavery. There Nativeism meant temperance to-day, abolitionism to-morrow and disunion the next day. They preserved their forms to act upon other societies, and to influence them to a merger with the parent organization, of which Mr. Seward was the Chief. They succeeded, and thus was swept out of sight an organization, which, a year or two before, had domineered over many of the States of the Union, North and South. This result of Native-ism in the North, of course, destroyed it in the Slave States.

The next step, in the progress of Abolitionism, under the leadership of Mr. Seward, was the absorption of the old whig party, a work which was accomplished at Syracuse, New York, in October, 1855. Two conventions were *arranged* to meet there—an abolition convention and a whig convention—avowedly for the purpose of making separate nominations for State officers, really for the pur-pose of signing articles of capitulation, on the part of the whigs, as a party, to the disunionists. All this was done in the most formal and technical manner. It completed the work of consolidation, so far as to embrace in the Abo-lition organization, every faction, interest and secret order, opposed to the democratic party.

The North was, then, with its solid New England majorities—its triumphs, the previous year, in New York, New Jersey, Pennsylvania, Ohio, Indiana, and Illinois, under the banners of abolitionism, perfectly organized against the Constitution. The arrangements to which reference is made, however, alarmed the people for the safety of the government. The elections of the following month, indicated the popular reaction, by withdrawing the great States of Pennsylvania, New Jersey, Indiana, and Illinois, from the conspirators.

[FROM THE NEW YORK HERALD, AUGUST 17, 1855.]

"In the history of American politics, there is to be found no such menace to the institutions of the country, as now threaten their early and complete overthrow. The first act of the conspirators is to place the Union of the States in complete subordination to Anti-slavery. The effort is to force on the country the organization of parties bounded by the free and the slave States, and to carry their points by the *numerical majorities of the North; to subvert the Constitution—to raise the power of such majorities into omnipotent control*, and then to plead the same in justification of their acts.

" It is a war upon the institutions of the South—a war upon slavery, and a war upon the Union, to effect the objects they have in view."

[FROM THE NEW YORK HERALD, NOVEMBER 18, 1855.]

"The distinctive Seward abolition party is essential disunion. It is based on principles whose tendency is, and whose effect must be, the destruction of the government and all its interests—its commerce, its railroads, its manufactures, its mechanic arts, its telegraphs, its moral power, and, above all, its position before the world as the representative of liberal ideas and popular rights. These are the sacrifices required of the American people to give effect to the Eutopian policy of Mr. Seward—to his *mad crusade against the Constitution*, with a *view of effecting his anti-slavery purposes*.

"The question comes home to existing party subdivisions with peculiar force : Can a citizen of the United States— an American—occupy any other ground than that of hostility to the Seward movement, and *do his duty to his country? That movement looks to a dissolution of the Union as a means to an end*. Those, then, who regard facts, and not forms, must see that in reality there can be but two parties in this country—those who support the government, *and those who seek its overthrow*. The abolitionists occupy one of these extremes ; the hards, the softs, the Americans, the whigs, in truth, occupy the other.

"It is manifest, indeed, that the public mind is gradually, but certainly, *approaching this one great issue*. It is natural, and, indeed, inevitable, that it should be so ; because it involves all the highest interests of the people, and in every sense must be regarded as the superior question of the day. In reaching it, individuals are required to pass the severe ordeal of putting their prejudices in subjection to their reason and their patriotism.

"Those who, without exactly knowing why, have come to regard the institution of slavery as a hateful sacrifice of the rights of man; those who have been taught to believe, that in the organization of the government, the slaveholders have secured undue advantages—in short, those who have stood upon the extreme North, and have listened only to partisan appeals and misrepresentations, in regard to affairs in the South, and have imbibed strong prejudices against the men and the local institutions of that section of our common Union, must make up their minds to see, hear, and give effect, to the truth, or consent to an early overthrow of the Union. The government cannot exist *in the midst of so much error.* *It must* fall by the weight of falsehood and misrepresentation; because these point directly to hostilities and civil war!"

[FROM THE HERALD, OCTOBER, 1860.]

"Put this republican party into the White House, and before it can be ousted it may compass the control of every department of the federal government. Then, the republican doctrine of negro equality would be apt to assume a shape so revolting as to 'precipitate the South into a revolution,' the terrible consequences of which would defy all human calculations. And so, for the sake of the Union, and the peace of the Union, the suffrages of all Northern men devoted to the Union should be cast in the way best adapted to defeat Lincoln, whose election will be an anti-slavery triumph which may drive the South out of the Union."

These warnings were regarded, when uttered, as mere alarms, intended to frighten the people, and lead them into the support of the Democratic party. We were all called, in derision, "Union-savers," and told that the South could not be forced into secession. The power of majorities was invoked, with an avowed purpose to provincialize the slave States! It was said, at the great mass meeting at Portland, in 1855, that the North must be educated, instructed, and, if need be, forced into Abolitionism—must be *taught* to condemn and despise the immoralities of the Federal Constitution!

It was these treasonable and emphatic declarations, in connection with previous acts, that led thoughtful men to the conclusion that the government of the Union was about to be sacrificed, and a new government created by the traitors, in its place. This has been accomplished, at a cost of men and blood, which no human power could have foreseen. As a work of slaughter, it is without parallel and beyond the means of explanation, except on the basis that slaughter is its policy and its triumph. It ordained a Revolution in the North, and has created a counter Revolution. It has conquered the North, and seeks the conquest of the South.

It is said there is no disease without a remedy. This maxim of medical science ought to be true when applied to political affairs. Where, then, is the specific for the frightful malady which has dethroned the reason and prostrated the body of the American nation? The future keeps its own secrets; the power of prophecy is not given to man, in such times as these. The mariner cannot take observations in the midst of the storm. We must, then, rely alone on the inborn freedom and bravery of the people of the States, to beat back the strong hand of power, which is now suspended over us. That this will be no easy work, we are admonished, by the fact that the people have armed the tyrants, not only by the sanction of legal forms, but placed the sword and the purse of the nation in their hands! Nine hundred millions of dollars have just been voted to them by a venal legislature. A million and a quarter of men have been sent to them by the States. All that men and money can do, to build up a central despotism, has been done; all that pride, insolence and tyranny can do, to make the people feel the power of that despotism, has been done by the existing administration. Every leading committee of the Senate is presided over by a New England man. Every measure of either House is dictated by New England men. The Army is controlled in all its appointments; the Executive Department is governed in all its details; the people are ruled over in all the various relations of life, by New England men. We have a Puritan system of politics, of police, of laws, of government, of everything. It is New England that governs New York, Ohio, and the great States of the Valley of the Mississippi! This Autocrat of Fanaticism is not satisfied to rule our political interests, but seeks to be our moral and religious instructor.

If these views are correct, they suggest an Armistice to the belligerents as the first great step in the way of reconciliation. The proclamation of such a measure would be received with intense joy throughout the country. It would suspend the agency of armies in the management of our political affairs, and restore the councils of peace and the influence of reason and patriotism, the only legitimate authority known to the institutions and habits of the American people.

www.ingramcontent.com/pod-product-compliance
Lightning Source LLC
Chambersburg PA
CBHW031823090426
42739CB00008B/1386